M... STORIES of the SAINTS

BOOK FOUR

BY REV. DANIEL A. LORD, S.J.

NIHIL OBSTAT: Arthur J. Scanlan S. T. D., Censor Librorum
IMPRIMATUR: Francis J. Spellman, D. D., Archbishop, New York

Published by:
William J. Hirten Co.
Cumberland, Rhode Island

Saint Agatha

THE PURE VIRGIN

Saint Agatha was very beautiful. People looked at her and said, "Oh, she is the fairest girl alive."

But Agatha was also very pure and good.

She loved Jesus Christ very much. She promised God she would never marry. "All my love is Yours," she said. "I will live and die for You."

Now it happened that the Governor of Sicily where Agatha lived heard of her beauty.

So he sent for her. Soldiers came and arrested her.

"You are a Christian," they said. "So you must go to jail."

"Dear Lord Jesus," she prayed, "I belong to You. Do not let this tyrant have power over me."

He made love to her. But she refused him.

So he threw her into prison. The governor was sure Agatha would be so afraid of prison that she would consent to love him.

Instead, she made the wicked woman who was her jailer love God too.

So the Governor ordered her to be tortured. She was not afraid. Then he ordered her to be beaten.

"Dear Jesus," she cried, "come and take me."

And Jesus came and took her home to heaven.

Her Feast is February 5th.

Saint Angela

FRIEND OF GIRLS

Angela de Merici was a lovely young Italian woman. She knew many poor girls.

Most of them did not know about Jesus Christ.

Many of them had never heard much about the lovely Mother of God.

Many of them were sinful and bad. But Angela knew this was because no one had taught them to be good.

So she gathered children around her and taught them about Jesus and Mary.

She helped sinful girls to become good once more.

She built houses where they could live and be safe from temptation.

She found fine, pure, wise young women to teach the children. She wanted sinless girls to help save sinful girls. She took Saint Ursula for her patron.

Then she invited good young women and pure, sweet girls to help her.

They became the first Ursuline Sisters.

They went all over the world teaching and helping little children and girls and young women.

Today there are thousands of these Sisters. They all call Saint Angela their Patroness and Holy Mother.

Her Feast is January 27th.

Saint Barbara

THE BRAVE MARTYR

When Barbara was a little girl, her wicked father imprisoned her in a high tower.

So Barbara lived in the tower with only the servants who cared for her. And she was very good.

One day a priest passed under her tower. He was singing about Jesus Christ. Barbara heard him. She asked him about his song. He told her all about the Savior. Barbara was overjoyed.

"I love Jesus too," she cried. "I am a Christian."

When her father heard this, he was furious.

In those days, it was against the law to love Jesus or to be a Christian. So this cruel father dragged his own daughter to the judge.

"My daughter is a Christian," he cried. "She is not my daughter any longer."

"What shall we do with her?" the judge asked. For he saw that Barbara was good and pure.

"Do what the law orders," her father shouted. "Beat her until she is almost dead. Then chop off her head."

So the soldiers carried out that cruel order.

But suddenly they saw angels coming. The angels carried the soul of Barbara to heaven. And a terrible flash of lightning struck her cruel father and killed him where he stood.

Her traditional Feast is December 4th.

Saint Bernadette

OF LOURDES

Bernadette' s mother and father were very poor.

One day Bernadette went to gather firewood. She came to a cave near a flowing river. Her friends played and sang. But Bernadette stood still, her eyes wide with wonder.

For she saw a beautiful Lady, who was dressed in blue and white. There were stars around the Lady' s head. Roses were on her feet. Bernadette told her parents and friends. At first they did not believe her.

But Bernadette saw the lovely Lady again and again. The lovely Lady ordered her to dig. A fresh, cool spring came bubbling up out of the ground.

Sick people who bathed in it grew well. Many of the blind could see again.

"Build here," said the lovely Lady, "a great church. And tell people to pray and do penance and walk in processions."

They did all this. Soon the wonderful Shrine of Lourdes was built.

And Bernadette waited until after the Lady had made her last visit to her. Then she went into the convent. She became a nun.

All the world knows about Lourdes. It is a beautiful shrine of Our Lady.

Her traditional Feast is February 18th.

Saint Brigid

OF IRELAND

When Brigid was a very little girl, Saint Patrick converted the Irish. She was a very beautiful little girl. Many young men wanted to marry her.

I shall be a nun," she thought. But she never knew she was going to be the first of millions of Irish nuns throughout the world.

"Make me ugly," she prayed to God. "Then I can love You alone."

God heard her prayer and she became very ugly.

With joy she became a sister, a nun. And as soon as she did, God made her more beautiful than ever.

She built a lovely little convent. She tended the cattle herself. Other young women heard about her. They came and asked to join her and be nuns too.

Then little girls came to be taught.

The sick came to her and asked her to care for them.

Often she sold everything she had and gave the money to the poor.

So the Irish called on her for help from all over the country.

So all over Ireland she went. She built convent schools and hospitals everywhere.

And when she died, all Ireland loved her. They made her the Patroness of the Green Isle.

Her Feast is February 1st.

Saint Catherine of Sienna
THE DOMINICAN

Catherine of Sienna was one of the greatest women that ever lived. When she was a little girl, our dear Lord appeared to her.

"Please give me your heart," He asked.

She gave it willingly. Jesus gave her His Sacred Heart in return.

Many rich young men wanted to marry this beautiful girl.

Instead, she became a Dominican Sister.

In those days, the Pope did not live in Rome. He had moved to France. Catherine went to see him.

"Holy Father," she said, "your place is in Rome. Come home to your people."

The Pope obeyed this simple little nun.

Many of the princes were furious. They did not want the Pope in Rome. So they tried to elect a false Pope.

Catherine, without fear, told them this was wrong.

They were afraid of her. They listened and obeyed.

The Pope knew she was very wise, and often asked for her advice. She always told him just what Jesus wanted and what would please God.

Although she was only thirty-three when she died, the whole world knew this saintly girl. They loved this brave woman.

Her Feast is April 29th.

Saint Clotilde

QUEEN OF FRANCE

Once upon a time there was a very beautiful princess. Her name was Clotilde. She lived in what is now France.

Many kings heard of her famous beauty. Each longed to make her his wife.

For Clotilde was as good as she was beautiful.

The strongest king of those days was named Clovis the Great. He was very warlike and often cruel.

He demanded that Clotilde marry him. So she did. But she was sorry because he was not a Christian.

His sweet wife loved him very much and he loved her. So he soon became less cruel. He was more merciful to his enemies.

Soon a powerful enemy attacked him.

"I will pray to Jesus for you," Clotilde said, "and you must pray too."

So they both prayed. And Clovis won a great victory.

He was grateful to his wife and to Jesus who had helped him. He became the first Catholic king of France.

When her husband died, Clotilde spent her time in prayer and in good deeds.

Her traditional Feast is June 3rd.

Saint Colette

THE FRANCISCAN

Colette lived in dangerous times.

Three men all pretended to be the real Pope.

Many Christians did not know which was the true Pope. But Colette did.

When she was a little girl she became a sister.

Saint Francis appeared to her in a vision one day. He asked her to love God very much.

"And make your sisters good nuns," he begged her.

So she did. She showed them how happy a good nun is. She taught them how to take care of the poor and teach little children about Jesus Christ.

This little nun loved the Catholic Church very much.

So God showed her which was the right Pope.

Bravely she told the Bishops and Cardinals what to do. They followed her advice. One Pope was elected and the Church was happy again.

The devils hated her because she was so good. They feared her because she loved the Church.

So they appeared to her in ugly shapes. They played horrid tricks on her. They tempted her severely.

"Stop praying to Jesus," they cried, "and we will stop bothering you." But she only prayed the harder.

She died smiling as she was praying to God to forgive all sinners.

Her Feast is March 6th.

Saint Genevieve

PATRONESS OF PARIS

Like Saint Joan of Arc, little Genevieve was a shepherdess. She tended her sheep near Paris.

One day a great saint passed by. He saw the little girl. "She is very holy," he said. "She will grow holier still." She spent her time in praying, in caring for the sick, in helping the poor.

A powerful king attacked Paris. The people were starving. Little Genevieve, quite unafraid, took some of her girl friends, and went out where the enemy could see her. They gathered food and brought it back to, the starving Parisians. No one dared to hurt her.

Another time, another general attacked Paris.

"Join with me in praying and fasting," she cried to the people. "He will not hurt us or hurt the city."

Everyone in Paris did as she said. To their delight, the general and his army packed up and left the city unharmed.

The new King of France had just become a Catholic.

Clovis was his name.

He heard about Genevieve and sent for her.

"Teach me how to be a good king," he asked this little shepherdess.

Paris loved Saint Genevieve. She is the city's patroness.

Her Feast is January 3rd.

Saint Mary of Egypt

WHO HAD BEEN A SINNER

When she was a very little girl, Mary of Egypt was a great sinner.

Almost everyone heard about her. For she was very beautiful. She led so many people into sin. She was very bad.

One day a crowd of people took ship for Jerusalem.

The king had just found the Cross on which our Lord was hung. Mary went along because she thought it fun to travel. She did not care about the Cross.

But when they came to Jerusalem, she went with the rest to the church. Inside was the Cross. She tried to enter. She could not. Some unseen force held her as if she were chained.

Suddenly, she knew how wicked she was.

She turned and saw a picture of Our Lady.

"Mary," she cried, "Mary Magdalen saw the Cross. Please let me stand beside that other sinful woman."

And she walked into the church. She knew that her sins had nailed Jesus to that Cross. She fell on her knees and cried and cried, repenting of all her sins.

Then she went out into the desert. For years she lived alone. She prayed. She did penance for her sin.

In the end, a holy man found her body on the sands. He buried the sinner who had become a saint.

Her Feast is April 9th.

Saint Martha

SISTER OF MARY MAGDALEN

Often our dear Lord was tired.

Often He grew weary when wicked men hated Him and tried to capture Him.

He would then go for a visit to His friends.

His friends were Lazarus and Mary and Martha.

They had a sweet and peaceful house in Bethany, not far from Jerusalem.

When He came to this house, He was happy.

Lazarus talked to Him. Mary sat at His feet and listened and loved Him.

But Martha was a busy little housekeeper.

She prepared the meals for our dear Lord.

When Lazarus, their brother, died, she and Mary sent for Jesus. All they said was, "The man You love is sick."

Jesus came Himself. In a wonderful miracle, He raised Lazarus from the dead. He gave their brother back to his sisters, Mary and Martha.

Martha was present on Calvary when Jesus died.

She helped prepare His body for burial.

She saw Him after He rose on Easter Sunday.

Later she and her brother and sister went to France.

They told the French about Jesus. Many of the Frenchmen and women believed and became Christians.

Her Feast is July 29th.

Saint Monica

MOTHER OF SAINT AUGUSTINE

Monica was a lovely young Roman girl.

She was wonderfully pure and good. She loved Jesus very much.

But her father loved money and power.

So he made her marry a young Roman who was very rich. Monica worried about her dear husband. She prayed hard that he would become a Catholic. She set him a good example. And a year before he died, he asked to be baptized.

But Augustine, her son, was her real worry.

Like his father, he did not care for the Catholic faith, and he led a wild and wicked life.

"I wish you would stop praying for me," he told her. But Monica prayed and prayed.

"Don't worry," a holy priest told her, "your son cannot be lost, not after all your prayers and tears."

So Monica followed Augustine to Rome. To her joy, she found that he had completely changed his life. He was a Catholic. He had given up his sins and his evil companions.

She thanked God. She died in peace knowing that her son was going to be a great saint and a great teacher and writer of Catholic truth.

Her Feast is August 27th.

Saint Matilda
THE QUEEN

Matilda' s father, a Saxon count, was named Theodoric.

Matilda' s parents wanted her to be pious. They placed her in the Monastery of Exford, where her grandmother was the Abbess.

There Matilda worked and prayed. She studied hard. She loved her work. She loved her parents. She loved her prayer and her spiritual reading. She became a model of virtue. Matilda' s parents gave her in marriage. Her husband became the German King and Matilda the Queen.

She was a good queen. While her husband went to war and enlarged his kingdom, Matilda won victories over spiritual enemies. She knew this was more worthy of a Christian. She was a pious queen. She helped the sick. She taught ignorant people about Jesus and helped them became Catholics. She spent much time in prayer and meditation, not only during the day, but far into the night. Finally, her husband helped her in her pious work.

When Matilda' s husband died, she called the priest to offer holy sacrifice for his soul. She cut off the jewels she wore. This was a pledge that she gave up, from that moment on, all pomp of the world.

Once there was a contest between Matilda' s sons, Otho and Henry. Matilda favored Henry, who was the younger son. For this fault, Matilda atoned by severe penance.

Matilda founded many churches and five monasteries. Her great pleasure was to teach the poor and ignorant how to pray. Matilda taught her people how to seek true virtue. "The beginning," she said, "is to want it and to ask it of God."

Her feast is March 14.

Saint Rose

OF VITERBO

Saint Rose was only eighteen when she died.

But she was already a holy and a famous person.

As soon as she could walk, she toddled straight to Jesus in the Tabernacle.

As soon as she could talk, she talked about Jesus and heaven and God.

There was a wicked king named Frederick in those days. He hated the Pope and made war on him.

One day some of his friends came to her city. They made speeches against the Pope. They threatened to do wicked things to him.

Little Rose was only ten years old.

Without fear, she rushed into the public square. She pushed the wicked men aside. She stood before the people of her city.

"Do not listen to these men," she cried. "The Pope is the Vicar of Jesus Christ. Love him and protect him."

The people were amazed at this little girl.

But they followed her and were true to the Pope.

When still a little girl, she became a nun.

Then she went to a little convent in her city. She prayed. She cared for the poor.

She died, and her body after death remained beautiful and fragrant.

Her traditional Feast is September 4th.

REGULA

Saint Scholastica

THE BENEDICTINE

Saint Benedict was the first of the holy monks.

Saint Scholastica was his beloved sister.

He built monasteries for holy men. She built convents for holy women.

Those were evil days and were full of dangers for good women.

Bands of wicked soldiers roamed all over the world.

So Saint Scholastica built lovely convents. They were full of peace. Women came there and were safe.

Saint Benedict loved his sister very much.

One day, he sat and talked with her about God.

Night came and he said, "I must go back to my home."

"Please don' t go," she said. For she knew she was going to die.

When her brother, Benedict, insisted upon leaving, she bowed her head and prayed.

Suddenly a great storm burst. The wind blew. The rain fell. The lightning flashed. Benedict could not go back. So all night long they sang together, they prayed together, they talked about God.

Three days later, Scholastica died. And Benedict saw her soul going up to heaven in the form of a pure, white dove.

Her Feast is February 10th.

Saint Teresa

THE CARMELITE

There were two great Saint Teresas.

One is called the Little Flower.

The other is called the Great Saint Teresa. She was the Holy Mother of the Carmelite Sisters. The Little Flower was one of her lovely spiritual children.

When the Great Teresa was a little girl, she ran away from home. Later she became a sister.

She grieved for all the sinners in the world who did not love God.

"I will love Him all the harder because they do not," she said.

"Dear God," she prayed, "forgive them. See! I will suffer and do penance for their sins."

So she slept on hard boards. She never ate meat. She prayed long hours.

She said to God, "Please let me love You. Please let me suffer for their sins. And do not punish the people who hate You and who are wicked."

Many holy young women joined her.

They prayed for sinners. They asked God to keep young people from temptation. They loved God like dear daughters.

And the Great Teresa built convents for them all over the world.

They are the Carmelite Nuns.

Her Feast is October 15th.

Saint Ursula

AND HER COMPANIONS

When Ursula was a little girl, she loved children very much. She therefore became a teacher.

Mothers and fathers sent their boys and girls to her.

She taught them how to be good. She told them about Jesus and Mary.

She had a fine school for them in England.

But terrible pagan armies came into England. They threatened to kill all Christians. So Ursula took her pupils and her other teachers and went with them to France.

But once again, she met peril.

The terrible Huns came with their armies. They hated Jesus Christ and they killed all Christians.

So they captured Ursula and her sweet young companions.

They asked Ursula to let them make slaves of the little boys and girls. Ursula refused.

They promised to let them all go free if they would give up Christ and the Catholic faith.

They all refused.

So the army of the Huns drew their swords. They pulled back their bows and arrows. They killed Ursula and all her companions. And like glorious martyrs they went straight to heaven.

Her Feast is October 21st.

Saint Veronica

OF THE WAY OF THE CROSS

We only know of one important incident in the life of Saint Veronica.

This took place on the terrible day of our dear Lord' s Passion.

Jesus was carrying His cross. All around Him the people were laughing and screaming. They were throwing mud in His face. They were spitting upon Him. They tripped Him and made Him fall.

Jesus looked around and saw no friends. Everyone seemed to hate Him.

Then Veronica came.

She just happened to be in the crowd.

She was timid and afraid, but she wanted to help Him.

So she took the veil off her head. She pushed the soldiers aside. She ran through the crowd. She came to Jesus. He had just fallen and He was too weak to stand up. Lovingly she wiped His face with her veil.

Jesus looked up gratefully. He thanked her with a smile. The soldiers pushed her away.

But when she got home and looked at her veil, she found a wonderful thing.

On the veil was a beautiful picture of Jesus. And Veronica kept that as long as she lived.

Her Feast is July 12th.

Saint Zita

THE LITTLE COOK

Zita was a little cook.

She worked in the kitchen of a rich family.

They thought she was just a drudge They piled work upon her. They gave her unpleasant jobs to do.

But Zita never complained. Early in the morning, she rose and hurried off to Mass. Then she returned, got breakfast for the family, and worked all day.

"Don' t work so hard,' the other servants said. "You make us ashamed of our laziness." So she did their work for them when they were tired and lazy.

One day she put the bread in the oven. Then she began to pray. She loved to talk to God. She loved to listen to Him. So she forgot her bread.

"Oh," she suddenly cried, "the bread will be burned." But it wasn' t. Angels had taken it out of the oven. And no bread had ever tasted so good or smelled so sweet.

The man and woman for whom she worked grew to love her. "Teach our children to be good like you," they asked her.

So she taught their children to be saints.

She was an old, old lady when she died. And the moment she died, a bright star appeared over the room where she had slept.

Her traditional Feast is April 27th.

CONTENTS

BOOK FOUR

Printed in Hong Kong